earthsong

april green

for my daughter

before the world got to claim you.
before you were clothed in material.
bathed in noise.
i held you.
a soul.
in my hands.

– earthchild

the dawn chorus:
birds telling mother
their dreams.

– earthsong

simple, soulful poems and haikus describing a
journey of survival; and the inescapable sorrow we
often endure before we understand why the birds
still sing every morning.

LOVING

a poem is
a reflection of a moment.
an echo of a memory.
held.
in the hand
of your mind.

– touched

there was no word
to describe being with you.
this was how i knew.
because. souls
don't use language.

how can it be…
he appeared out of nowhere; yet
i had known him my entire life.
he felt like a place i had visited before.
a land i remembered.
a language i used to know.

– soul mate

it is rare...
to find a person
you can reveal
your hidden self
to.

— once

wait...
take off my body
it's weighing me down.

– love me *now*

he loves me
in the same way
the moon loves
the night sky.

— holding her up in the darkness

– halo

you will know
when i love you.
i love with the same
silver light
as a falling star.

his eyes changed colour
when he looked at me.
like a flood of light from his soul.
it was as though i was the moon.
pulling his blue ocean towards me.
and always, in those silent seconds,
i would hear the crest of a wave.

— falling in the distance

— every atom

and i loved him. all of him.
even the shadow falling
behind him like a smudge
of ink from his bones.

his voice finds me
through the air and
i hold it in my hand
like a whisper
against my skin.

he didn't compare me
to the moon.
he compared me
to her reflection.
parting the ocean in two.
bleeding her golden essence
across the water.

– goddess

i want you to read my mind.
there is poetry inside me.
there is ink in my blood.

— write me

— delicate

there was a beautiful silk thread
running through us.
like a ribbon bound into a book of sacred verse.
unmoving... untouched.
buried between pages dipped in gold ink.
like the blood in our veins.
like the pulse of the words.

— one

i have worn you all day.
on my skin. in my mouth.
in every sense.
i have become you.

and when i see him
all the poems inside my
body start dancing.

— our world

being without him made me homesick.
not so much for him. but for me.
for the person i became when i was with him.
for the piece of earth i belonged to
when i was with him.

and my love for you hurts.
the way the moon bruising her flesh
as she falls upon the horizon
hurts.

do you feel
my heartbeat
when you think about me?

the light from his eyes
tangles around my body.
and i come undone.

i carry the essence of you
in the hand of my heart.
like strawberry stains on fingers.
sweet nectar running through my veins.

– how do i ever remove you?

your love letter:
unfolding like the dawn.
a fragment of light in my hands.
i read until the blue ink becomes your eyes.
until the words become your touch.
until the silence floods the room
with your presence.

— our language

april green

i have loved you all day

i remember
i used to climb inside him
and lie amongst the clouds.
inhaling the scent of belonging.
the taste of another world.
and i would watch the silver lining
beneath his skin; moving with his breath.
rising
like a silk parachute.
falling
like a sprinkling of stardust.

and i never found another place like him again.
i never found another world like him again.

– home

silence
and you.
and this air.
heavy
with anticipation.

like the weight of rain
before
it touches you.

i wear you in my eyes.
everything i look at
is dressed as you.
disguised as you.
even when asleep.
you appear to me.
out of the blue.
dressing my body
with the skin of
thin air.

nights when we spoke in silence.
the kind of silence only our souls
understood.

i will give you things.
from the inside... from my heart.
just open me up.

you look at me
and it is simple, yet –
it is falling through the sky.
and
swimming in the ocean.
and
tasting a memory.
and
missing a future.
and
breaking my heart.

– all at the same time

we loved in secret.
in folded poems
tucked into spines.
carved into bones.
and tears. like
falling ink. like
strings of pearls
coming undone.

— the unraveling

why do we
sometimes
choose pain
long before
we experience
it?

every tear i cry is a poem.
falling from my body.
wanting to be written.

— poetry in motion

can we dance
in my darkness
for a little
while?

i gave a lifetime
of love to you
in an hour.
unaware
it would take
a lifetime
of hours
to undo.

— the unfastening

sometimes,
our lives are made
more painful
by love.

we talked about greek myths.
about helen...odysseus.
but never about the tragedy
that was unfolding between us.
never about the war we were
about to start.

— the passion

the last time he looked at me.
the light from his eyes
touched my ashen skin.
like a sacred promise.
like a delicate kiss.

– eternal

– the homecoming

before you go –
press your scent onto my soul.
let your essence find its way back to me
in another life.
because this life is but a borrowing of bodies.
so i will meet you in the place where time and
flesh no longer exist.
where the sky becomes the sea.
where the moon becomes the earth.

my heart breaks in two
and thousands of stars shatter
in the distant sky.

GRIEVING

– alone

my days are without shape.
a dress worn too often.
a shadow obscured.
i try to sharpen the hours
but even the scissors
are blunt.

i pray
for something
to steal the pain
from me as i sleep.
the way the night
steals salt from the
sea and scatters it
across the sky.

no letter today.
only the sound of my heart
folding up inside.

the eyes were
cleverly designed
to protect us
from ever seeing
our own tears.

– swimming ghosts

and when the rain comes;
dropping the sky onto my
skin... i can taste you.

how kind nature is:
holding our pain
in her arms
whilst we sleep.

– mother

the stars string together
pearls from moonlight
and leave them on my
pillow for morning.

– prayer beads

– without you

the force of your
presence weighs
heavy on me.
sometimes, more real
than you ever were.

my fragile heart;
wrapped in
memories,
delicately
tied with the
string of our atoms.

— and this is how i carry you

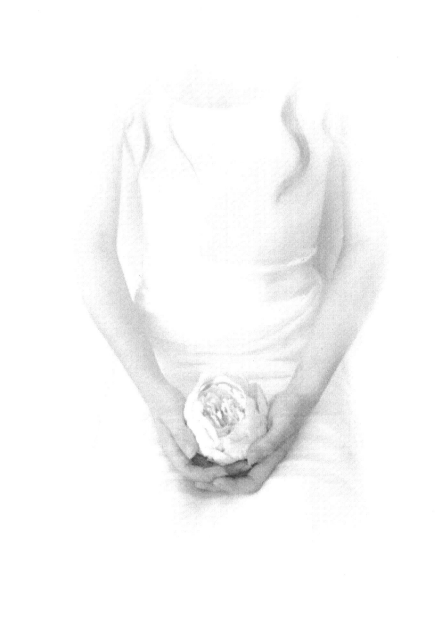

will you always be
this ache inside me.
this empty space that
i fill with silent tears?

i love you as though we invented the sky.
i still dream that you will one day break through
the seam of a cloud and come and find me.

– living gifts

if only we could
treat people as though
they were the dead
returning to us...
how different
our relationships
would be.

it is a brave act –
to be alone with
memories.

— unreachable

i can still hear your voice.
echoing from the last
place you spoke to me.
like a chill in the air.
like an ache in my bones.

i miss the silence
between us. it's too quiet
now that you have gone.

– eternal moment

i can bring back to life
every detail of that hour with you.
the one where we spoke in silence.
where time stood still.
and we forgot.

the rain is breaking
inside my mouth
and silence is swelling
in my throat;
like a heart
holding too much pain.

nights when i feel
this timeless silhouette
settled between ribs.
like feathers; fallen
from time.
a broken and familiar
language.

— heartbeat

you're always here.
always here in
a different language.
a different light.
a different song.
but. always here.
running through
my bones.

i will wait for you.
like the sand
waits for the sea.

— come back to me

i will meet you in our language.

i often wonder
if some of the
tears i cry
are yours.

— falling from the sky

a dream about you -
it never leaves me.
it lives within me.
an emotional imprint
on my soul.

— stained

the way loss
embeds itself into your bones.
like a shadow.
forever reminding you about
that which is missing.

your love –
it was the only thing
i never questioned.

there are days when i can't speak.
when my own voice startles me.
echoes through my shell.
haunts my sleeping bones.
like a sudden cry. like a lost child.
these are the lonesome days.

— the days when you are most upon me

i have lived
many years
without you
yet i know
you more
now.

language and breathing
and silence
are not enough for all that
i have to tell you.
it's that place in between
where the moon rises in our bones.

– meet me there

it is in a chamber
of my heavy heart
that i hold all the things
i have lost.

— spare room

sometimes my
handwriting falls out
of your books and
my spine breaks in two.

— letters from me

time hangs
like a heavy velvet curtain.
like silent darkness;
only changing with the light.
never moving... never drawing back.

— grief

i still breathe you.

i know you exist...
deep in the earth.
we still speak
the same
language.

– mother tongue

days when i love the air
because it carries every atom
of you.

— fingerprints

i still have the poetry book you gave me.
the pages are turned down
and i'm afraid to look inside.
afraid to read the words.
touch the paper.
find fragments of you there.

i found a feather.
it touched my skin like a kiss.
i know it was you.

— ether

no matter how far back we go.
we can never draw all memory
out of our bones. out of our hearts.
for we leave fragments of memory
all over the world.
in places we have loved.
in places we have left behind.
like pieces of thread
clinging
to the universe.
drawn into the air.
pulled into the sea.
always returning back
to us
with the wind and the tide.

– the pain of grief

it is always caused by love.

we are all the same.
we have just loved
different people.
wept at different graves.
but. we are all the same.

– one

DYING

i write
to bring all
that has died in me
back to life.

there is a soul.
there is a body.
there is an ego.

— there is confusion

i was alive
when i was a child.
i was a free spirit.
a soul with a body.
...i died
the minute
i realised
i was a human.

— ego kills

— the wolf

i am forever haunted
by the echo living
within.

— the dwelling

sometimes. when there is no hope on the outside. no path we wish to follow. we find some land within. we build a shelter and we decorate it with our own type of material. our own type of love. we paint images on the canvas of our bones. and we hang them on the walls of our hearts. and over time. this once baron land becomes a home. and we live there. unmasked. as our true selves. and in this eternal place. death is not a stranger to us. for we died to the outside world many years before.

— the other

you will never rob me
of my mystery.
for even she
is a stranger to me.

sorrow made from silk tears
dresses my broken bones.

sadness hangs within me
like the faces inside
a silver locket.
carried around the neck,
heavy against the heart.
never opened.
never seeing the light.

— locked inside

when will you realise –
i am not the years
behind you.
i am here.
in front of you.

– now

we break people in half
looking for answers.
as though they were
carved into their bones.

– hieroglyphics

the deeper i drown
when i think about all the things
i let slip through my fingers.

— like rain when the storm came

— mirrors

we fought
because i was at war
with myself.
you were never
going to win my battle.

i understand this now.

that quiet thing i do...
i'm listening.
to my soul.
i want to know
if she remembers
you.

— another life

i am restless here.
the moon is tugging my soul.
the stars want me home.

do not measure me
from head to foot.
for that would be
like searching for the
corners of the ocean.

– depth

there is so much
distance between us
that our words
sound broken
before they are
even heard.

— misunderstood

i want a simple love.

— with profound depth

some days
it is always night.
day after day.

— always dark

– the hidden life

behind every voice
is an echo of a world
we know nothing of.

i can see darkness in others
because i have lived so long
without light.

— compassion

i am certain that
some of my deeper
scars are inflicted
upon myself.

– soul searching

i have always had that faraway look in my
eyes. i have spent my entire life gazing into
space. searching. wandering. looking for a
land i remember. a land that remembers me.
it sometimes feels as though the moon is
tugging at my soul. drawing me closer.
whispering to me. charging me. like a piece of
amethyst. reminding me to keep looking up.
keep looking up.

wherever you are.
i pray you don't
feel the pain that
shapes and haunts
my flesh.

– the living

— missing piece

i was born
with a hole in my soul.
it is where the darkness
climbs through.

— the injured bird

it was not self-pity.
it was catching a glimpse
of myself and wondering
what you would think
if you were still here to see.
the feathers had fallen off.
a wing was broken in two.
the flesh was torn apart.
it was pity for you.
not pity for me.

i am difficult to love
because
i keep a part of me hidden away.

– even from myself

— black as night

there are some nights
when even the moonlight
will not brighten
the darkness within.

dependence
on something
other than your heart
to make you happy
kills your soul.

the past is concealed
in a memory
i can't always
remember.

— compulsion

there is no greater agony
than being pulled
towards something
your heart is begging
you to stay away from.

some desires eat you whole.
spit you out.
leave you with a gaping wound.
hungry for more.

other desires. feed you.
make you whole.
leave you with a piece of treasure.
hungry for more.

— carnal vs pure

we mistake so much for love.
and
so little for self-abuse.

i am often distracted
by moments
that did not even
belong to me.

love me
in the space of my being
where it is most dark.
for there is a lonely
sense of longing
hidden there.

— broken wings

collecting feathers
to remind myself who i am.
as though they have fallen
from time.
as though they are missing
from me.

the fragile pieces
returning home.

my love for you
was undivided.
it was you.
over me.
over anyone else
over anything else.
it was you.
it was always you.

– obsession

forgive my quiet.
but there are days
when i need
to hear
my own
language.

– in silence

we shape our future
on everything that has
never happened.

— waste of time

i would have forgotten
by now
had it not been
for the scars.

— permanence

it is hard.
keeping the
two worlds
separate.
this is what
heartbreak is.

– this is broken in two

and what happens
when the mask
starts needing
a mask?

– who

my tears always turn to ink.

sometimes,
we hide our truths outside
in the open
for everyone but ourselves to see.

— cry for help

— hidden

wounded memories never seem to lessen with
the passage of time. if anything, they grow
heavier. like rocks under the sea. impossible
to lift without drowning. and i fear that
bringing them to the surface would disturb
them too much anyway. so they live here. in
my body of water. weighing heavy on my soul.
and this is how i carry them.

some people.
they look at me
and i know.
my blood feels the torment.
my bones bear the pain.
the compulsion.
the self-loathing.
the withdrawal.

— the others

— the blue room

don't let the living
us your mind as a graveyard.
the dead should be your only
visitors.

SURVIVING

when i leave this cage.
when i fly without your grip.
what will i become?

you knew the truth
long before i did.
you whispered it
my whole existence.
like a fragmented song.
like a broken melody.
pain taught me to listen.
love translated the words.

— higher self

over-exposed
i wait for you in darkness.
only the light teaches me
who you are.

— the saviour

and now that i have
faced my truths.
i can face my true
reflection.

— unashamed

some scars only silence can carry.

they ask
what it feels like
to be free.
and i tell them.
the cage door
isn't locked.

— fly

never disown your darkness.
for that would be like a rose
renouncing her roots.

– guardian

an ancient peace
descended upon me today.
settled into my broken bones.
lit up the darkened spaces.
like a luminous layer of love.
like a veil of holy water.

i know why she came.

she came to carry me.
to remind me about my future.

without you all year
i finally see the
seasons change.
i see golden
dresses of wood
hanging on the trees.
and the veil i embroidered
with my own hands.
fallen.
like a scorched leaf.

— clarity

— the invisible cage

there are moments
when my mind sits in empty space.
like a captive of the air.
like a bird paused in flight.
unmoving.
unbound.
forgetting for a second.
and it is here. in these moments.
when i am the most free.

— the calling

a memory of home
keeps haunting me.
a whispered voice
flutters within.
like the delicate motion
of a birds feathered
wing.

– earthsong

the alchemy of the earth.
the remnants of feather and bone.
flowers and bark.
the scent of sweetness.
of memory, that keeps us alive.

for years
i was searching
for a land i remembered.
a language i understood.
and then. in solitude.
i found it.

— within

the deepest part
of the wound
holds the most
light.

— black heart

arriving home
i realise i had
never really left.
i was just living in
a different chamber.
a darker room.

a broken person
knows how to put themselves back
together again.

HEALING

sit amongst these words
for a while...
there is healing between
the silent spaces.

— sacred

— self-destruction is a creative act:

when you want to run away and start again.
when your mind is crowded with the voices of
others.
with interference.
with conditions.
with inherited beliefs.

when the chaos becomes too much and you
start craving flight and abandonment.

this is when you self-destruct.

you think it is madness; but it is not.
it is creation.
because it is the creative force within you
that blows the hole in your structure.
and it blows the hole in your structure so that
inspiration can step in and fill it.

then you become a phoenix — rising from your
own ash.

'do you still break?'
she asked.

'sometimes,' i said.
'but it's softer now.
it doesn't hurt as much.'

listen to the earth
when she speaks softly
to you.

this thing you are feeling.
this insecurity.
this imagined flaw.
find it. find out what
is feeding it.
what is keeping it alive?

– you

it will come.
and it will heal.
and it will leave.

it is you who keeps re-visiting it.

— pain

mother yourself

– own the ground

you must know this.
you have a place here.
on the sacred ground.
in the hallowed wind.
this is where you belong.
this is where you have
always belonged.

even on the darkest
of nights. the light
still shines in places.
hold out your hand.

— look closer

you must weep.
you must weep like the sky.
because tears are like rain.
softening all that has hardened.
preparing the earthly body for fresh fruit.
loosening the flesh for the soul to grow.
how else can it be released.
how else can it be freed to heal your pain?

— the unfolding

if the bleakness of
winter enters your body
plant snowdrops within.

we make amends
by ending
the war within.
first.

— surrender

this feeling of trying to fit in. stop. you will
send your soul into exile. be yourself. embrace
yourself. love who you are. don't try and
change. come home to yourself. and when you
do; the chaos in your heart will settle. your
soul will show you what comfortable in your
own skin feels like.

(comparison may be the thief of joy but
conformity is the thief of life)

— she was a star

because she was drawn to the darkness.
not just in herself. but in other people too.
and when she touched them.
they all shone together.

growth happens
when the darkness
is most upon you.

— spring bulb

when the load is lightened.
when the flesh is removed.
the core shines through.

– illumination

i like the way you
look at me.
something i remember,
something i used to know
them.
like the language

show me a damaged person
and i will show you
a poem in their bones.
a painting in their blood.
a song in their heart.

— art amongst the ruins

a gentle touch
can keep a person
from disappearing
into themselves.
it can save them.

– it can save you

there is pain.
before the poem.
like a wound
before it heals.
and then.
the words...
they become
fading scars.

– the healer

sometimes,
we violate our bodies.
our very own flesh.
instead of searching
within our souls
for that which
we can heal.

earthsong

we think things
come to stay.
but really.
things come
to pass.

– this too

a p r i l   g r e e n

to my body:
i give you back
all that i have
taken.

— forgive me

wear your scars as jewels.
for they were messengers
sent to heal the greater
parts of you.

– the gifts

we do not really change.
we just shed all illusions.

(unlearning is the greatest gift
we can be taught)

— strength and dignity

some scars are still unborn.
wear them with honour
when they arrive.

– wholeness

the unique.
individual.
creative.
parts of yourself
will forever haunt you
unless you embrace them.
unless you love them.
own them.
nurture them.

and when you do;
when you close the circle around them.
you will be whole.

for how else can you be whole,
if you do not own all the parts?

just because you are damaged
does not mean you are
undeserving.

— remember this

— i want to tell you something:

do not follow the crowd.
do not unconciously eat their words.
your soul will die.

you are unique.
there is no other footprint like yours.
walk your own path.
choose your own life.
the one that is whispering through your
bones
like a haunting melody.

don't change for people.
just change the people you are choosing.
choose the passionate ones.
the mad ones.
the ones who set your soul on fire.
the ones who stop time.
the ones who suspend you in the air like
captured dust every time you talk to them.

and.
spend time alone. be happy alone.

find things that nurture your soul.
nature and art and books and cafes and.
little things. it's the little things...

to be the poem
running
through your veins.
the ink
beneath your skin.

— i would write you the whispering words
of your soul

i want to be like the moon
and touch you through the
darkness.

in order to heal any kind of pain,
you have to do something very
few ever do.

– talk about it

(even if it's just to the air.
talk about it.
whisper it.
let it drift out of your being)

at the root of your problems
are people who feel exactly the same.

— find them

and the bravest part
of the endless sorrow
is to walk through it.

because only here,
will the roses bloom.

my soul unfolded
like a lotus flower and
then i understood.

– my heart

once strangled by thorns,
rises like a climbing rose.
like a graceful queen
taking her crown.

there is something
reassuring about being
back in the womb
of the earth...
every new flower
becomes your child.

– re-birth

listen...
you are telling yourself
what you want.
you are standing
in the answer.

— inner voice

— the meeting of the soul

how beautiful:
to finally understand that
solitude
is a mark of self worth.
to truly accept that you,
alone,
are worthy of your own company.

find your own voice.
you do not even have
to speak.

— art

don't leave this earth
with words still inside you.
songs unsung.
canvases untouched.

– what if?

we are human stars.
we carry eternity
within us. always.

she was trapped
inside my ribs
so i broke them open
and
let her go.

true beauty
is not given. it is grown.
within.
true beauty lives in the
lining of your skin.
in the essence of your being.
in your very soul.

to know this.
to embrace this.

is to be beautiful.

— when you are healing:

set some boundaries.
do not let them treat you
as you were.
do not treat yourself
as you were.
you are stronger now.
you are healing.
re-inforce yourself with a boundary.
it is not a wall.
it is soft.
it is protecting
you.
because —

you did not dig your soul
out of the dark
to hand it to someone else.

when your mind is still.
when your lips are silent.
your heart plays a thousand
songs.

— in harmony

poetry
without emotion
is like a body
without
a soul.

it is a power —

to be yourself.

notice the harmony
when people share
the same passion.

their souls sing
together.

on days
when you are hurting –
stay as gracious as an angel
with a broken wing.
shine
without ever rising.

– this is amazing grace

if i could –
i would collect your
abandoned dreams
(balancing on the edge of regret)
and i would bring them
back to you.

i opened my heart
to look for pieces of you.
and i found myself.

remember –
it is your heart.
only you can nurture it.
only you can make it
bloom.

– the seeker

when you find your passion
you will realise it was there all along.
you will realise that it has found you.
and you will smile at the calling.
at the song that has been singing
within.

she gathered up all of her broken pieces
and hung them in the darkness like stars.
and each one wrote her a poem.
a letter.
a song.

i found these words
in the darkness.
they were inside me all along.

— i wrote them for you

and in the end.
we always go back
to the beginning.

– circles

the following few pages are taken from my illustrated poetry book "paper wings."

thank you for your love and support.

love april green

come home to yourself.
your soul has tales
to sing.

— broken wings

to the self–loathers. the self–fixers who seek
anesthetic in everything they touch. the ones who
keep a whole language inside the lining of their
skin, which flows fluent like a river in their veins
and doesn't ever stop.
the ones who don't want to feel the pain but when
the numbness becomes too much; want to feel it
one more time in order to forget it one more time.
the ones who hate themselves for what they keep
doing to themselves but keep doing it to
themselves because they hate themselves.
the ones who can't see a way out because they
have fallen too far in.

please believe me – there are other people out
there who feel exactly the same as you do.
find them.

'i can do this on my own' is denial because the way
you are harming yourself is showing you that you
can't. so you have to get on your knees and tell the
air that you can no longer do this alone.
you have to find the strength to fall.

that's when something will step in and carry you.
that's when something will slowly put you back
together.

but you have to ask. you have to ask.

because some battles can only be won
by surrendering.

if the pain
is not going away,
then you are not
listening
to what it is telling you.

— the other side of silence

tell me about
the other side of silence.
for i have this inexplicable hunger
for something my hands can't reach
but my soul longs for.
and it is not of this world.
but i have known it.
i have felt it;
stepping over my ribs
like a flightless bird.
it is a hunger for something
that never comes.

if i am not enough for you
then you are not enough for yourself.
you have a hole in your soul
that only you can fill.

do not depend on me
to make you feel better.
do not ask me to fill your hole.

— i am busy filling my own

that's the beautiful
thing about self-love –
you wear it like a dress
and it becomes more and more
exquisite
with time.

i will return to you
wrapped in moonlight
and dust.

instagram & twitter: @loveaprilgreen

Made in the USA
Columbia, SC
26 August 2017